America Reads
College of the Siskiyous
800 College Avenue
Weed, CA 96094
530-938-5345

Treasure Hunt

D1016851

Treasure Hunt

*10 Stepping Stones to a New and
More Confident You!*

Pam Grout

SkillPath Publications
Mission, Kansas

Project Editor: Kelly Scanlon

Editor: Jane Doyle Guthrie

Cover and Book Design: Rod Hankins

ISBN: 1-878542-97-4

10   9   8   7   6   5   4   3   2   96   97   98   99

Printed in the United States of America

"I have more confidence than I do talent, and I think confidence is the main achiever of success."

— *Dolly Parton*

Contents

Beginning Your Treasure Hunt

Every blade of grass has its angel
that bends over it and whispers,
"Grow, grow."

—*The Talmud*

If you think you just bought a book, the joke's on you.

If you actually think you're going to sit down in an easy chair, maybe pop open a Coke, and then read this like you have hundreds of other books, well, you better think again. In fact, you should be warned right now that this is not an ordinary book. Anymore than you are an ordinary person.

This book, if you will, is actually a commission. Your own personal commission. If you choose to accept it (and the fact that you're reading these words right now is a pretty good clue that you're ready), you're at the brink of a genuine treasure hunt. If you thought Christopher Columbus and Marco Polo set out on pretty interesting journeys, just you wait. This book is going to take you places those two never thought about going.

If you stick with this treasure map and follow all the stepping stones, you're going to end up with an extremely valuable treasure—worth more than all the gold in Fort Knox, all the oil in Kuwait, even all the diamonds in Liz Taylor's jewelry box. Yet you won't find it on any commodities chart. Unfortunately, very few people even know about this treasure. It stays covered by years and years of erroneous thinking. It's often hidden under a sea of fear, a river of doubt, a whirlpool of remorse. For many of us, this incredible, one-of-a-kind treasure gets completely submerged under old tapes, under niggling feelings of self-doubt, under layers and layers of distorted beliefs that just aren't true.

The good news is the treasure is still there.

It's you.

Not some you that you've manufactured to please your parents. Or your spouse. Or your boss. Or your tennis partner. This you, this self, is the one that was planted in your heart on the day you were born.

You, in all your covered-up glory, are absolutely unique. Of all the billion humans that have walked this planet, not one has been exactly like you, nor will anyone ever be. This blueprint gave you an important assignment, a special hole that only you can fill. In the big scheme of things, the universe needs you to contribute your own personal piece of the puzzle. There is something you—and only you— can offer.

The passing years and perhaps some decisions made in the name of "security" have buried your sense of all this. If you've started this search before but came up feeling empty-handed, maybe you weren't digging in the right place. Or maybe you stopped short when you struck fool's gold.

The exercises you'll work with and play with in this book are each a specially planned leg of your journey toward self-discovery. Some may seem like "day trips"; others may take you halfway around your inner world. Although the stepping stones that make up this treasure hunt are offered in a suggested order, you'll not see any timelines or deadlines or schedules anywhere. After you finish each one, in an afternoon or a month, go on to the next at your own pace and pleasure. You may even want to tackle some of them with your spouse or a special friend.

Tools for the Hunt

No self-respecting treasure hunter would try to "dig around" without a set of tools. Just as the surgeon needs a scalpel and the tennis pro a racket, the treasure hunter needs proper equipment too.

You probably already have much of what you need, but if not, you can easily pick up most at any discount store. And remember, you're worth this investment of time, energy, and expense.

Make sure you have these tools:

- A spiral notebook
- A pair of scissors
- Some sheets of colored paper
- Markers
- A small, pocket-size travel alarm clock
- Your library card (renew it if you've let it expire)

The Record of Your Journey

Ten stepping stones will make up your treasure hunt. Use the "Record of Your Journey," bound in the back of this book, to tick them off as you do the exercises and reach each one. Or if you prefer, buy yourself some gold stars to stick on the map as you cross each point of passage.

Whatever you do, don't just read through this book and throw it on a pile with all your others. Sure you've got important things to do. But in the long run, what's more important than you? If someone guaranteed you'd win the lottery if you followed the steps laid out here, you'd do it, wouldn't you? Remember, the treasure you will uncover here is far more valuable than any lottery winnings. It's important to acknowledge yourself and to believe you deserve this effort. You do!

Stepping Stone 1.

As a
Man
Thinketh

It is the mind that maketh good or ill, that maketh wretched or happy, rich or poor.

—*Edmund Spenser*

Thoughts are powerful things. Every facet of our lives is strongly determined by what we think about ourselves. People who think they deserve success, friendship, and happiness tend to attract it. Likewise, those who think they don't deserve it seem to attract mostly failure and unhappiness. Their plans never quite work out.

For example, you may have heard about a skinny kid from Austria who was teased by his playmates. One day, fed up by the constant ribbing, he decided to change his thoughts about himself. He spent many hours visualizing the success he craved. He began to believe that he was worthy, and this provided him with the energy and focus to take on a serious body-building program. Eventually, he won the Mr. Universe title, moved to America (another big part of his dream), and in time proceeded to star in and produce many successful movies. He even went on to marry a woman from one of America's best-known families. That skinny Austrian, as you may have figured out by now, was none other than Arnold Schwarzenneger.

But, but, you may be thinking, he's a big, big Hollywood producer. He's the Terminator. I'm just small potatoes.

Dig this.

Andrew Carnegie started out as a day laborer making 28 cents a day. Eventually, he gave $465 million to the American Library system. Goldie Hawn was once a go-go dancer, Clint Eastwood was a busboy, Willie Nelson was a church choir director, and Barbara Bush, in her recent biography, said, "I was so shy. I once cried over having to speak to the Houston Garden Club."

The point is simple: Everybody has to start somewhere.

Even those who make it aren't immune from self-doubts. David Darling, a former member of the Paul Winter Consort and a world-renowned recording artist, gives music workshops. At these workshops, he has a rule that if a negative thought comes up, something like, "Oh, man, I'm not musical" or "I'm doing it all wrong," you're supposed to ignore it. Tap yourself on the head, but ignore it. Before long, participants look around the room and notice everyone tapping themselves on the head. And his workshops are attended by many very successful musicians—Bobby "Don't Worry, Be Happy" McFerrin, for example, and Peter, Paul, and Mary.

Remember, you're not alone. Everybody thinks they're short of the mark from time to time.

Now, get the alarm clock from your stash of

treasure-hunting tools. Over the course of several hours, set the alarm to go off each hour. When it does, ask yourself what was bobbing around in your mind. Write it down in the Thought Diary on the next page.

When you've completed the diary, analyze what you wrote down. Were you thinking about what a great person you are and how much you're enjoying whatever it is you're doing? You'll be amazed to discover the thoughts you have about yourself. Always pay attention to the messages you're giving yourself. Are you talking yourself up, or are you usually running the old "I can't" record?

Pat yourself on the back for completing this exercise, and don't forget to give yourself your first gold star.

Thought Diary

As your alarm goes off each hour, quickly jot down the thoughts running through your head. No fair editing them—write them down as accurately as possible.

1st Hour: _____

_____

_____

_____

_____

2nd Hour: _____

_____

_____

_____

_____

3rd Hour: _____

_____

_____

_____

_____

4th Hour: _____

_____

_____

_____

_____

5th Hour: _____

_____

_____

_____

_____

_____

6th Hour: _____

_____

_____

_____

7th Hour: _____

_____

_____

_____

8th Hour: _____

_____

_____

_____

Check off Stepping Stone 1.

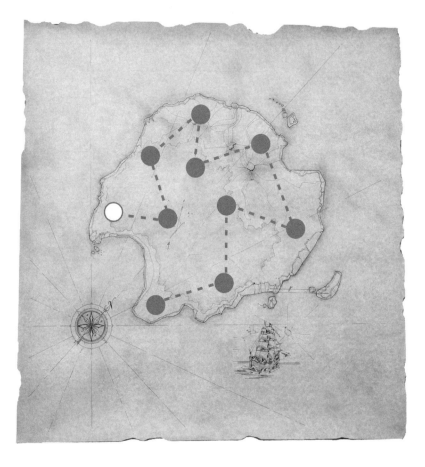

Stepping Stone 2.

Dig
Through
Fear

We have nothing to fear but fear itself.
—Franklin Delano Roosevelt

Okay, it's time to get out an imaginary shovel. The first layer that's hiding your treasure is fear. In fact, most of us are so afraid of fear that we don't even acknowledge that we have it. That's what this stepping stone is all about.

Fear causes us to limit our horizons, to stick to things that are "safe" or unchallenging. We stay in jobs that are beneath our talents. We don't attempt to write those books that we know are in us. We don't speak up at company meetings. In other words, we regularly and totally sabotage our chances of finding that precious inner blueprint.

It's like driving a car with the brakes on. Think how ridiculous it would be for an Olympic runner to strap on a 25-pound weight belt before starting a race. Without realizing it, though, we often move through life with our brakes partly set. The horsepower is there, but vast areas of potential are blocked, bottled up, restricted from effective application.

When we take a good honest look at our fear, it can melt away like snow in the sunshine.

Get out your spiral notebook and write down this root sentence:

"A fear I have about being myself is
_____."

Now fill in the blank, maybe with something like the following:

"A fear I have about being myself is nobody will like me if they see who I really am."

"A fear I have about being myself is I'll lose my nerve if someone disagrees with me."

"A fear I have about being myself is that people will think I'm from outer space."

Don't judge what comes up. Just write it down. Nobody is going to read this but you. Don't stop until you've listed at least twelve fears about being yourself. You may end up with many more than that—just let your thoughts flow as freely as possible and write them all down as quickly as they come. And for heaven's sake, don't be concerned about how precisely you express yourself, or the niceties of grammar and sentence structure. The only object here is to get your fears onto the page.

Here are a couple of suggestions to facilitate the process:

1. If you can't think of anything, make something up. You'll get warmed up and before long, you'll be writing down some of your true fears.

2. Don't judge the reality of your fears. When something comes to mind, don't question it. Write it down anyway.

The object of this process is to let go of your fears. And you do so by releasing them from your mind and capturing them on paper. Many of our fears hide just out of reach of our conscious awareness. Even if we're aware of them, we still may look at them as little as possible and keep them a secret from others.

We do this for a perfectly logical reason: Acknowledging our fears might make them real. There's only one thing wrong with that line of reasoning, though—it happens to be completely false. Owning and acknowledging fear is an enormously effective first step in letting go of fear and disempowering it.

It's the fear that we refuse to acknowledge, the fear that we bury under a blanket of denial, that has power over us. And the only power it has is what we give it by refusing to look it straight in the eye.

Unacknowledged fear takes on a variety of forms: hostility, anger, exhaustion, depression, an inability to concentrate. It has the capacity to cut us off from our true selves, from taking necessary chances. It contributes in innumerable ways to the process of self-sabotage.

Now, get out a bright piece of paper and write this statement on it:

> "I am now willing to act in the presence of fear. I hereby resolve that I will never again allow fear to keep me from doing something I genuinely desire to do."

Now sign your name, write down the date, and place the sign on your desk, your bathroom mirror, or some other prominent place.

And don't forget to check off Stepping Stone 2.

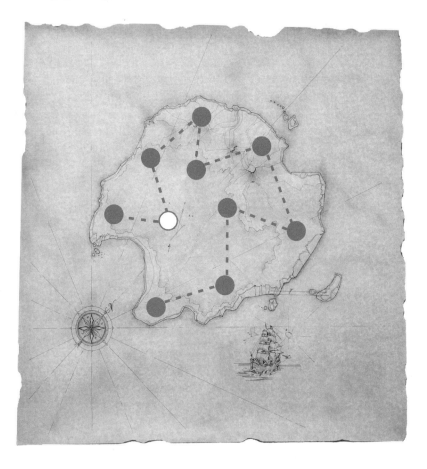

Stepping Stone 3.

Reprogram Your Inner Computer

There is no value judgment more important to man—no factor more decisive in his psychological development and motivation— than the estimate he passes on himself.

—Nathaniel Branden

Your thoughts and fears about yourself are like computer software. Although your mind (the computer) has been programmed quite effectively and will continue to run the old software as long as you leave it alone, you can always change the status quo—much like you can replace a word processing program such as WordStar with another such as WordPerfect or Microsoft Word.

So how do we reprogram our thoughts? Needless to say, we can't get rid of strong, deep-rooted programming by simply willing it out of existence, especially when we've operated for perhaps many years on the basis that it was gospel truth.

The solution: to create a new program to replace and contradict the old one. This stepping stone is all about using affirmations. A good affirmation for you might go something like this:

"I, your name, am good enough just the way I am."

Someone described an affirmation as nothing more than a strong positive thought that we implant in our consciousness with the intention of producing results in our lives. Affirmations enable us to let go of negative programming and make room for a more positive variety. And when used in the following way, affirmations can also be powerful tools for self-analysis: you can use them to discover disempowering negative thoughts you never knew you had.

Here's how the process works. Open to a page in your spiral notebook and draw a line down the center. On the left side, write your affirmation. Then, without thinking about it, jot down on the right the first response that pops into your mind.

Now write your affirmation again. And in the right-hand column, write down another response, not the same one as before.

What you end up with might look something like this:

Affirmation	**Response Column**
I, Jean, no longer need to worry about failing.	But if I don't, who will?
I, Jean, no longer need to worry about failing.	I've got to worry. It's a family trait.

After you've written the affirmation five times with a different response, switch to the second person, like this:

You, Jean, no longer need to worry about failing.	I don't?

Note that last negative response. As you take yourself through the process, a little ray of sunshine eventually creeps in.

Now, switch to third person:

Jean no longer needs
to worry about failing.

Don't bother with a response column the last time
you write the affirmation. Allow yourself to end on a
positive note. You might also want to cap the series
by returning to the first person and writing the
affirmation five more times without a response
column, just to drill in that upbeat finale.

Remember, immediately after you write your
affirmation each time, write the first response that
comes to mind. Don't stop to figure out whether you
really mean it or whether it really applies. Just write
it down. If you can't think of a negative response,
make one up! Don't leave the space blank. If you
do, your mind will seize that as an escape clause
and be "unable" to think of responses on other
occasions. Make sure you produce a response every
time.

By using the negative response column, you turn the
process into something worlds apart from simple
positive thinking. It's not enough to drill positive
thoughts into your mind, not if you're still holding
onto negative thoughts that keep you from believing
them. To do so is like trying to keep breathing in
without ever breathing out. You have to exhale to
make room for the next inhale.

Do affirmations really work? Can such a simple process actually enable you to change the nature of your mental programming?

In a word, yes.

The process is really quite remarkable, and one of the most rewarding aspects is that you can actually see it work. The negative response column provides you with a window to the workings of your mind.

As you work with a particular affirmation over a period of weeks, you'll notice a change in the nature of your responses. Certain thoughts that were powerful immediate reactions at the beginning eventually won't come to mind at all. When this happens, you'll know you've been increasingly able to internalize new beliefs about yourself.

Eventually the affirmation will go flat for you. It will no longer get an emotional response.

Here are some other things to know about affirmations:

1. *They should always be in the present tense.* "I am ravishingly beautiful" is better than "I am going to look good someday."

2. *They should always be in the active voice.* "My success pleases me and everyone else," not "Others are pleased by my success."

3. *They should be positive rather than negative.* "I am confident and secure" is better than "I am not that insecure."

4. *Give them some punch.* Instead of "I know I possess the skills necessary to obtain the success I want by using affirmations," try "Affirmations make me successful."

5. *They should be brief.* Long, flowery affirmations with dependent clauses trailing off in all directions may appeal to your poetic impulses, but they don't get the point across to your brain. By the time you finish the sentence, your mind has lost track of the beginning. Make your declarations short, direct, and to the point.

If an affirmation upsets and irritates you, that's not necessarily a bad sign. The part of you that's bothered by it is the part that doesn't want to let go.

Watch out for the other bugaboos that might get in your way:

1. *Saying affirmations don't work.* The cure? "All my affirmations work miracles for me."

2. *Avoiding the process altogether.* Try this affirmation: "I now enjoy writing affirmations."

3. *Believing that affirmations are brainwashing.* Just remember that you chose the first thoughts that created your reality and it's up to you to choose others.

Following are some tips for succeeding with affirmations:

1. *Experiment.* Substitute one of your nicknames from childhood when you write your declarations. For example, if you were called "Scooter" until you were eight, use that instead of your "grown-up" or business name: "I, Scooter, enjoy meeting new people." Or if your first language isn't English, try writing affirmations in your native tongue.

2. *Don't try too much at once.* One or two affirmations at a time is fine. Try writing them twice a day—twenty times in the morning and twenty times at night. Try too many and your mind will get confused.

3. *Stay with each affirmation for a few weeks.* You have to give yourself time to change your thinking.

4. *Let negative responses guide you.* Negative responses are not cryptograms containing all the secrets of the universe, but they definitely hold lessons that deserve attention.

5. *Don't beat yourself up when you don't do them.* That defeats the purpose.

And finally:

1. *Use an affirmation as a mantra.* Run it over and over in your mind. Say it to yourself when you're doing dishes or when you're driving.

2. *Say it out loud.* Sit in front of a mirror and gaze into your own eyes while you say it.

3. *Decorate your house with it.* Copy your affirmation onto several index cards and hang them up at strategic spots around the house.

4. *Make a tape of your own voice repeating your affirmation.*

And, of course, tick off Stepping Stone 3 on the Record of Your Journey.

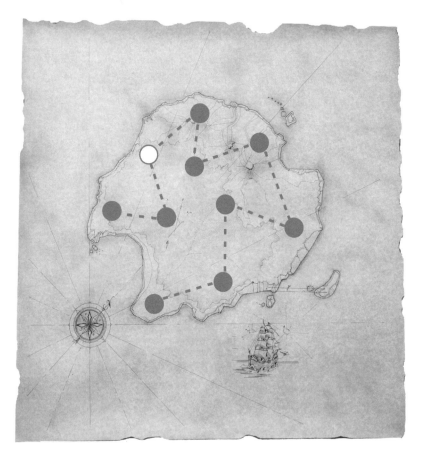

Stepping Stone 4.

Plato Said
It Best:
Know Thyself

*You need to claim the events of your life
to make yourself yours.*

—Anne Wilson Schaef

If you really knew who you were, you'd never have reason to doubt yourself. But unfortunately, many of us are so busy conforming to the goals and ideals we inherited from our parents or our second-grade teacher that we've forgotten who we really are.

It's important to claim your life as your own, though most of us don't very easily. We're too busy keeping up with the Joneses, wearing the perfume that Calvin Klein told us to wear, or listening to the music that some Top 40 chart said we should like. This is where the real "you" gets buried.

Another challenge to owning your own life is today's pervasive mass media. We all watch the same TV shows and read the same newspapers with stories from the same news bureaus. Learn to decide for yourself what you like and don't like, to form your own opinion, rather than let advertisers or political analysts tell you what it should be.

Right now, today, it's time to "get a life." That's the whole point of this treasure hunt. To find out who you really are. To honor that special person. While Stepping Stones 3 and 4 worked on fear and old programming, that's only part of the picture. You also learn about yourself by figuring out who your favorite baseball player is or by telling someone your secret dream.

Popular self-help books talk about "owning your childhood" and healing past hurts. Sure, your inner child may have been wounded, but he or she also dreamed of magic and made castles out of sand, right? Why spend all your time working out the depressed, hurt part of you when the inner magician is just as real, just as present?

Maybe you'll already know the answers to the self-exploratory questions that follow. If so, you've undoubtedly discovered the richness of your own life. Most of us, however, couldn't respond right off the top of our heads—we've never sat down long enough to think about much that's uniquely important to us.

A couple of pointers: If you can't think of an answer, do a little library research. Maybe you'll have fun finding out who your favorite president is. Maybe you'll learn so much about the American political system that you'll end up running for mayor. Get out your spiral notebook, and feel free to write one word, a paragraph, or a whole book. Maybe you'll even end up on the bestseller list!

Here you go:

1. What's your favorite constellation? planet? kind of cloud?

2. When was your first visit to the doctor?

3. What sport would you like to be good at?

4. What's your favorite city? What do you like about it? Maybe it's a certain Polish breadmaker, or the fact that all your cousins live there. Or maybe the magnolia trees are gorgeous in the spring.

5. What's your favorite building in town?

6. Who is your favorite poet? (This is where that library card will come in handy—if you don't know, go find out!) Remember, some people consider songwriters like the Indigo Girls and Bob Dylan to be modern-day poets.

7. What's your favorite river? tree? flower? Don't forget to ask yourself why you like these things. The answers may reveal great truths to you.

8. What are you good at? Don't overlook things like building friendships or making banana bread. Maybe you're exceptionally good at keeping the peace, or at making others feel wonderful about themselves.

9. What's your favorite color?

10. What was your favorite book as a kid?

11. Who was your favorite president? (Is that library card burning in your pocket?)

12. What's your favorite letter? number? shape?

13. In the movie *The Way We Were*, Robert Redford's character and a friend spent an enjoyable day naming their favorite day. What was your favorite day? age? grade in school? (Remember to ask yourself why.)

14. What would you name a boat if you owned one?

15. Who was your favorite cartoon character when you were a child?

16. What is your nickname? What nickname would you like to have? What would you nickname a co-worker?

17. What's your favorite card game?

18. What movie would you like to see made?

19. What do you think an angel looks like?

20. Who is your hero?

21. What do you think of questions like these? Why?

Now that you've come up with the answers, do you see a thread running through them? Have you discovered anything about yourself? Remember the quote that started this stepping stone: "You need to claim the events of your life to make yourself yours."

Check off Stepping Stone 4.

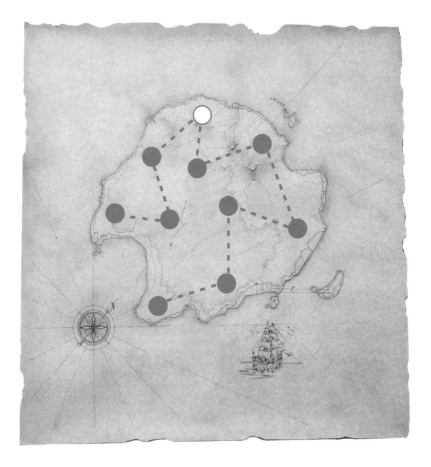

Stepping Stone 5.

Dare
to Be
Mediocre

*A man's mind stretched by a new idea can never
go back to its original dimensions.*

—*Oliver Wendell Holmes*

Now it's time to dream. You've faced your fears, and you're ready to act on some of the interests you've discovered. Maybe you're about to launch a new hobby, or try a different job. Who knows? As the TV host said, "This is YOUR life."

The task here is to let your imagination soar without bumping its head on your need to be perfect. Let's start a new exercise with an open-ended question:

"If I knew I didn't have to do it perfectly, I would try
_____."

Here are some examples:

1. Taking a watercolor class

2. Performing stand-up comedy

3. Playing water polo

4. Reading my poetry in public

In your spiral notebook, make a list of at least twenty such things. Then choose one—and do it. Forget about being perfect—do it just for the pure enjoyment of doing it.

Check off Stepping Stone 5.

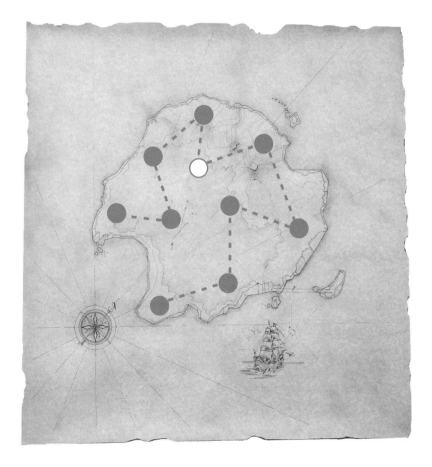

Stepping Stone 6.

Take an Inspiration Break

*They are like the clue in the labyrinth,
or the compass in the night.*

—Joseph Joubert

By now you probably need a break from writing and thinking and inching along that Record of Your Journey. On this stepping stone, then, you're going to draw on and connect with somebody else's wisdom. You're going to collect a basketful of inspiration. Next time you're wondering why you're bothering to try to like yourself or change your life or even get out of the bed in the morning, you can refresh yourself by reading through this collection.

Go to the library or consult your own sources (books, tapes, music recordings, a letter from a friend) to find at least a dozen quotes that speak to your heart. Write them in your spiral notebook or maybe paint them on a sheet of pretty paper.

Here is an example:

> "What lies behind us and what lies before us are tiny matters, compared to what lies within us." — Ralph Waldo Emerson

Remember, this exercise is all about you. Pick out quotes that you like. That way, when you feel your confidence slipping, you can read them and reaffirm what you believe about yourself.

Okay, get out your pen or your gold stars and tick off Stepping Stone 6.

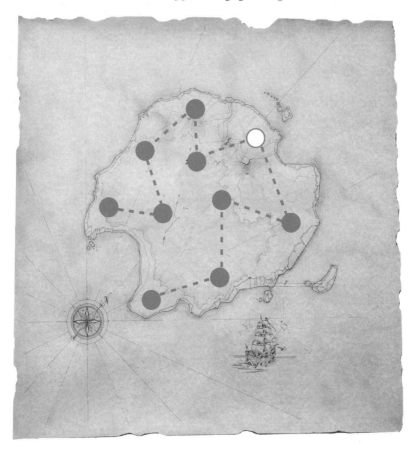

Stepping Stone 7.

Create
a
Legacy

*You know very well that love is, above all,
the gift of oneself!*

—*Jean Anouilh in* Ardèle

Now that you're relaxed and better at examining who you are and what you want out of life, how about having some fun?

As you've seen over and over by now, the main point of all these exercises and stepping stones is learning to honor your life—getting in the habit of celebrating the unique specimen of humanity that you and only you are. To do this, this stepping stone lays out a series of nine "legacies" for you to create. These exercises are similar to the questions you answered in Stepping Stone 4, just a bit more detailed. They'll probably take more time, but you'll end up with something you can use for life. Perhaps one of your "legacies" may even result in a business opportunity.

Don't take these exercises lightly, but also don't feel like you have to finish them by tomorrow. Remember, this is a treasure hunt, not a test or a job. Although it may take you ten years to complete your search with this book, just know that every moment you spend on these exercises should present joyful, exciting realizations of the wonderful person you are. Are you ready?

Legacy 1:
Ancestry!

What do you know about the country from which your family hails? What's the story of your ancestors? If possible, plan a trip to go there. Perhaps you still have distant cousins there.

Think of Alex Haley. He became a household name when he sat down and dug up his ancestry. Your "roots" are just as interesting. *How to Trace Your Family Tree* by the American Genealogy Research Institute is a book you might want to check out to help you get going.

Legacy 2:
Create your own personalized stationery.

Why buy someone else's idea of who you are when you can make your own? Many important missives will come from your now-fertile mind and open heart. Make the look of your stationery stand for or symbolize you in some way (Would you choose a bicycle? a garden tool? a vibrant combination of colors?). Just as most businesses have their own stationery, think of your new business as "Me 101."

If you want to make your own paper, check out Tonia Todman's *Paper-Making Book.*

Legacy 3:
Become an expert at something.

Think of some subject that you're fairly interested in. Maybe it's Tasmanian devils. Or making art from recycled egg cartons. Or growing herbs or programming computers. It doesn't matter how large or small the topic—it's just important to be passionate about something. Are there other people interested in this subject too? Maybe you can join a club. Or start one!

Legacy 4:
Create something that's uniquely yours.

For example, maybe you'd like to create your own signature scent. Don't start making excuses, something like: "But I have my own signature scent. I always wear White Shoulders or Giorgio." If there weren't several other hundreds of thousands who also buy and wear the perfume, the company would no longer be in business.

Why not make your own cologne or perfume? There are several places where you can custom order your own perfume. For starters, contact Essences at (617) 859-8009.

One woman started collecting herbs in the forests of Connecticut and ended up launching her own herbal bath company.

Another suggestion is to create your own sandwich. There's a deli in New York that sells Woody Allens and Burt Reynolds and many other sandwiches named for famous people. Each sandwich is either named after the person who likes to order it, or it reminds the owner of that person for some reason. At any rate, all these celebrities have their own sandwich.

You don't have to make it to Broadway to have your own sandwich. What do you like? One woman who loved sweet potatoes and bean sprouts created her own sandwich with sweet potatoes and bean sprouts. What's your favorite bread? Maybe you like pita or you make a sensational cranberry bread in your own breadmaker.

Or maybe you'd rather decorate a hat or paint some tennis shoes that say "you." Anybody could take one look at those hats or shoes and say, "Those must be Jean's (or Joe's or Mary's)."

Legacy 5:
Invent something to make your world better.

There's some pet peeve that's been bugging you since you were twelve—the paper carrier who throws the paper in the bushes or coffee that doesn't stay warm very long. C'mon, something's bubbling up inside your brain about now.

You don't have to actually make the device that will solve the problem—although you might want to—but do come up with some solution to this nagging problem. For example, if you want your coffee to stay warm longer, maybe you could design an insulated mug or a heater to plug it in to.

One woman hated the way her pet always bounced around when she took him to the vet. She invented doggie seat belts that, at last report, were selling like hotcakes. *People* magazine even wrote a story about her.

Legacy 6:
Create a family crest.

Back in their ancestral country, most families had a crest or coat of arms. It often depicted the family's line of work or their special attributes (such as courage or valor) or whatever made them stand out. You can design your own crest. Don't try dodging this with an excuse like "I can't draw." Keep the spirit of the exercise in mind and keep it simple. Make a mosaic if you need to.

Legacy 7:
Write your own life story.

"It is in the knowledge of the genuine conditions of our lives that we must draw our strength to live and our reasons for living."

—*Simone De Beauvoir*

To give you an example, Iris DeMent, an internationally-known folk singer, wrote a touching story about her father on her last album cover.

She talked about her dad being a fiddler who gave it up when he "found the Lord." Iris was always curious about her father's fiddle and one day, when she was seven or eight years old, she found a box in her parent's closet. Sure enough, it was the fiddle. She dragged it down and stared at it for quite some time.

She goes on to tell the story of her dad's introduction to the fiddle. It wasn't a family story until he was already old and already in a wheelchair. He told how his own father had bought it and promised it to any son who could reach it on the wall and play it.

Although Iris's father was too small to reach the fiddle, he did study his brothers playing it. One day, he begged to play it. He did and was told right then and there that it must be his fiddle.

Now, it's your turn. Your life is just as interesting as Iris DeMent's. Tell us about it.

Legacy 8:
Find your own special place.

In the book *The Education of Little Tree,* a story about a Native American boy raised by his grandparents, Little Tree was advised to find his own special place. His grandmother told him, "This is where you go to feel alive, where you feel the closest to God." Your place might be a park or a mountain near your home. It might be a coffeehouse where you can sketch pictures of the other customers. It might be an overstuffed chair in your den where you can wrap yourself in a favorite old afghan. The only criterion is that it be a place that you feel is all yours when you're there, where you can find the peace and quiet to think and enjoy your own company.

Legacy 9:
Write your own personal credo.

Many businesses and organizations create a beliefs statement to set standards and a focus for their employees or members. It's the way the group says "this is what we're about." Articulating your own beliefs or what's important to you by writing a personal credo can help you prioritize things, make decisions, and better see your "niche" in life.

As an example, here's an excerpt from a poster created by San Francisco-based artist SARK:

> "Stay loose. Learn to watch snails. Plant impossible gardens. Invite someone dangerous to tea. Make little signs that say 'Yes' and post them all over your house. Make friends with freedom and uncertainty. Look forward to dreams. Cry during movies. Swing as high as you can on a swingset, by moonlight. Cultivate moods. Refuse to be responsible."

SARK also believes in wearing pajamas to work, taking naps, and drawing on walls. She concentrates every day on what she calls her life's mission: to free creative spirits everywhere. What's your life's mission?

Whatever you do, don't forget to tick off Stepping Stone 7.

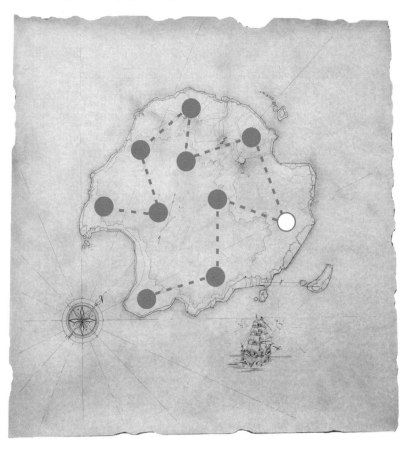

Stepping Stone 8.

Collect Ammunition Against Negativity

A misty morning does not signify a cloudy day.

—Ancient proverb

Face it. There are going to be days when you feel like leftover mashed potatoes. This is when you need to call up the reserves. You need help.

It's okay to prepare that help ahead of time. Collecting ammunition comes in handy when your inner critic rears its ugly head. You know, that voice that says you're not good enough to sing at the company party or you're not educated enough to get that raise.

This is where we wage war. Because no matter how good you get at liking yourself, this critical monster will come sneaking back in. It's very crafty (having been with you for a long time) and it's not booted out easily.

Negative thoughts have helped keep you from having loving relationships or from writing the book you've always wanted to write. In fact, negative thoughts may be the only thing keeping you from being the next Rod Stewart. Have you ever considered that the main difference between you and any superstar may be that unlike you, the star believes he or she deserves to make gold records and draw millions to sold-out concerts?

On the following pages are a few ideas for positive ammunition. See which ones resonate for you. Whatever you do, though, arm yourself with at least three.

Ammunition:
Visualize eliminating your inner critic.

Picture using a giant eraser to rub out that negative voice when it starts whispering in your ear. Or imagine tossing it into the basket of a hot air balloon and then letting the balloon sail off into the stratosphere.

Ammunition:
Create a library of inspiring books.

For starters, try anything by Og Mandino, Ralph Waldo Emerson, or, if you're into ancients, Marcus Aurelius. You already have a list of quotes from Stepping Stone 6—see what else these great thinkers said. Ten minutes with a great classic or any other source that makes you appreciate the magnitude and glory of life can work wonders for your mental attitude.

Ammunition:
Write down every good thing you can remember anyone saying about you.

Remember that old girlfriend who said you were greater looking than Paul Newman and Robert Redford combined? Or that former boss who said you had no idea how talented you are? Write these morale boosters down and pull out the list when you need to.

Ammunition:
No matter what happens, always remember you have a choice.

You can choose either to get frustrated and mad or to look on the positive side, viewing the proverbial glass as half full rather than half empty. Next time life deals you a setback, decide to change the one thing you do have control over—your attitude. A setback, no matter how devastating, is not going to last forever.

Ammunition:
Reframe your problem.

See difficulties as opportunities for growth and self-mastery. Even simple word choices can make a big difference. A "problem," for example, is nothing but a "challenge." Be "for" something instead of "against" its counterpart. Say "yes" instead of "no."

Ammunition:
Get some exercise.

A brisk walk around the block can do wonders for your attitude. SARK, the artist mentioned in the last stepping stone, takes "miracle walks." Here's how she describes one in *Inspiration Sandwich:* "Wear a brightly-colored hat and pick a destination that delights you. Along the way, communicate with every animal and child you see. Notice colors. Stomp in every puddle. Follow your insight. Peer over fences, sit on a park bench. Bring a notebook or sketch pad and position yourself in some extraordinary spot."

Ammunition:
Look for someone to praise.

Complimenting others can't help but make you feel better about yourself. You'll feel good for uplifting someone else, and you'll turn your focus from your problem du jour to another person.

Ammunition:
Watch an uplifting movie.

Don't reserve *It's a Wonderful Life* just for the holidays! Pop some popcorn, pour a glass of your favorite beverage, and settle into the most comfortable chair in the house. No fair doing work, folding laundry, or paying the bills while you watch the movie. This time is for *you.*

Ammunition:
Make a list of 100 things you want to do before you die.

Tape it to your mirror and read some part of it every morning. Choose one item and develop a strategy for achieving it. Set a realistic time frame. Some items may take years to come to fruition, depending on their nature and what's involved. The important thing is to set the wheels in motion *now*.

Ammunition:
Get some much-needed solitude.

Sit on a park bench or take a walk by yourself. If you're like most people, you're so busy attending to the self-imposed "shoulds" of your life that you rarely take time for yourself. You get so busy running errands and doing favors for other people that you forget to check in with Number One, to reflect on what you want. According to psychologist and author Bruce Baldwin, everyone needs an hour each day for leisure pursuits.

Ammunition:
Write a love letter to yourself.

C'mon, you can't claim to have never written one before. Not even to the cute guy or girl in your seventh-grade algebra class? Maybe you've never actually sent one, but you've composed one—at least in your mind. Now's the time to whisper sweet nothings into your own ear. You're the one you have to fall in love with. You're the one who matters now.

How you feel about this exercise will tell you heaps about yourself. Did you resist doing it? Did you resent doing it? Did you think, "Why bother?" That attitude could represent the way you treat your body, your time, and your entire life. What do you love about yourself? Your sense of humor? The report on guitars you wrote in the fourth grade? Now's the time to shine. Why not buy a card or use some of your personalized stationery. Make it really special.

Okay, it's time to tick off Stepping Stone 8.

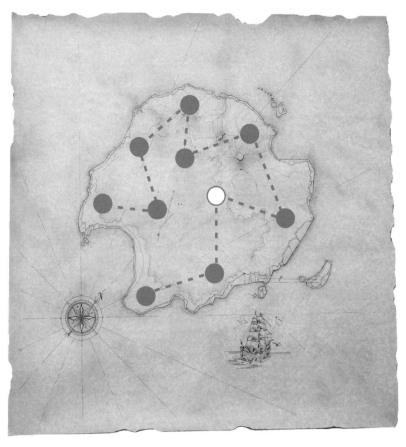

Stepping Stone 9.

Count
Your
Blessings

*"What a wonderful life I've had.
If only I'd realized it sooner."*

—Colette

Remember that what you think about manifests itself in your life. It's very important to appreciate all you have, all you are. Sit down right now and write down 100 things you're grateful for. Such a list will greatly improve your perspective. If you're feeling so lousy that you can't think of anything, consider these powerful gifts—and they're only a small sampling of the many you possess:

Can you see? Can you watch the radiant sun rising every morning? Can your magnificent eyes witness the miracle of tiny buds on a tree, a bird gliding in the wind, a mighty canyon carved by a meandering river, the graceful silhouette of a swan, a baby's smile?

Can you hear? Can you listen to your favorite radio station, your favorite records, your loved ones telling you they care?

Can you speak? With your words, you can soothe the pain of an injured child, encourage those without hope, say "I love you," and inspire others to action.

Can you smell? Close your eyes and inhale deeply through your nose. Imagine the fragrance of spring flowers. The cologne of someone you love. The earthy smell of rain on a spring day. You could smell them all, couldn't you? And the smells weren't even near. What powerful gifts we all have.

The more you are grateful, the more you will learn to love your life.

Get up every Monday morning and write down ten things you're grateful for. Write them on the bathroom mirror in soap. That way, they'll still be there for you when you go to bed and get back up again all week long. It's better to look in the mirror and see what you're grateful for than to feel sorry for yourself.

Now, tick off Stepping Stone 9.

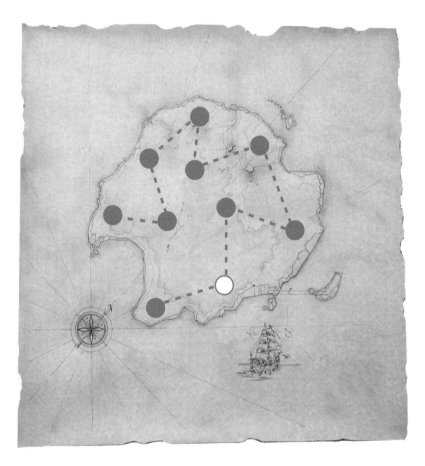

Stepping Stone 10.

Try Something Playful or Spontaneous

My goal is to say or do at least one outrageous thing every week.

*—Maggie Kuhn,
founder of the Gray Panthers*

Tapping into your sense of fun and spontaneity is a great defense against negative thinking. Doing so regularly also limbers up your mind, keeping you receptive to bursts of insight and creativity when they drop in unannounced.

For starters, stand up right now—wherever you are—pretend to toot a horn, and proclaim: "I am a masterpiece. There is no one like me."

Here are some other things to try:

Go to the fanciest hotel in town and sit for a while in the lobby. SARK used to go to the St. Francis with her pads and paper. She'd put up a sign that said "Take an artist to lunch." And people did.

Remember the hokeypokey you used to sing at the skating rink or at weddings? Do that. It's important to get energy moving through your body.

Every day go on a walk in a different fun place, indoors or out. Try some public gardens or a lavish neighborhood or even a college campus if you haven't been back to school for a while.

Head for the hot tub or run a deep, warm bath. Get in and feel the sensations over every part of your body. Splash around and sing if you like. Feel the warm water healing you, nurturing and resurrecting your spirit.

Go out and buy yourself a gift. It doesn't have to be expensive. Perhaps it's a packet of grape Kool-Aid. Or a 59-cent bubble maker. Maybe you want to splurge and buy a handsome tennis racquet or a new coat. There *is* some special something that you'd love to have. (And remember to remind yourself you're worth it.)

- Wear your pajamas to the movie theater.

- Learn a card trick.

- Sign up for Spanish lessons.

- Memorize three clean jokes.

- Give to charity all the clothes you haven't worn the past three years.

- Feed a stranger's expired parking meter.

- Visit that enticing junk store down the street.

Check off Stepping Stone 10.

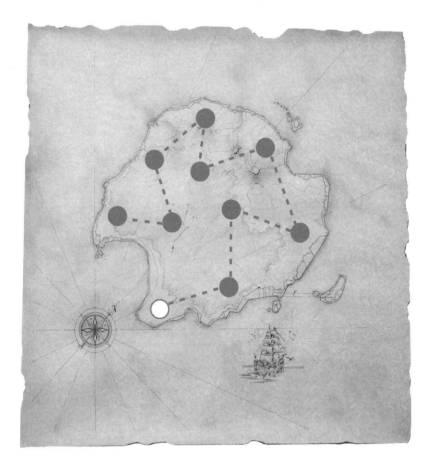

Finding
Your
Treasure

*The farther back you can look, the farther
forward you are likely to see.*

—*Winston Churchill*

You've heard the adage, "Life's a journey, not a destination." Meaning that we learn, change, and grow every day. Essentially, that's what this treasure hunt has been about—changing, growing, getting to know—and like—yourself better as you followed the path laid out by the ten stepping stones.

And so, with each step you took, with each bit of insight you gained about yourself, with every moment of growth and self-revelation along the journey, you discovered yet another piece of your treasure.

You learned how to replace the negative thoughts that distort your self-image and tear down your self-confidence. What's more, you confronted the fears that keep you from stepping forward and asserting yourself.

Armed with this positive sense of self, you learned that it's actually okay to own the events of your life, to acknowledge their contribution to making you what you are today. You learned to embrace your assets and the things, people, and events that make your life rich rather than dwell on past hurts and failures. Then you went one step further and created a legacy to celebrate the unique person that you are.

Finally, you collected basketfuls of inspiration to give

you strength and to help you ride out life's occasional jolts, to give you the energy and fortitude to move further up the beach and start over again on days when the tide's too strong and washes away your sand castles. Most important, you learned to forgive yourself and move on when you make a mistake.

Look now at the Record of Your Journey. Where are you? Back at the beginning, your new beginning, ready to continue your lifelong journey of self-discovery, secure in the wisdom and confidence you acquired on this leg of your trip. Happy traveling!

Bibliography

American Genealogical Research Institute. *How to Trace Your Family Tree: A Complete and Easy to Understand Guide for the Beginner.* Arlington, VA: American Genealogical Research Institute, 1973.

Branden, Nathaniel. *How to Raise Your Self-Esteem.* Toronto: Bantam Books, 1987.

Briles, Judith. *The Confidence Factor: How Self-Esteem Can Change Your Life.* New York: MasterMedia Limited, 1990.

Briley, Richard Gaylord. *Are You Positive? The Secret of Positive Thinkers' Success.* Washington, D.C.: Acropolis Books, 1986.

Butler, Pamela W. *Talking to Yourself: Learning the Language of Self-Affirmation*. San Francisco: Harper & Row, 1991.

Carter, Forest. *The Education of Little Tree*. Boston: G. K. Hall, 1992.

Givens, Charles J. *Super Self: Doubling Your Personal Effectiveness*. New York: Simon & Schuster, 1993.

McGinnis, Alan Loy. *Confidence: How to Succeed at Being Yourself*. Minneapolis, MN: Augsburg Publishing, 1987.

McWilliams, Peter and John-Roger. *You Can't Afford the Luxury of a Negative Thought*. Los Angeles: Prelude Press, 1991.

Newman, James W. *Release Your Brakes! To Get Where You Want to Go Faster... The PACE Owner-Operator Manual for the Human System*. Thorofore, NJ: Charles B. Slack, 1977.

SARK. *Inspiration Sandwich*. Celestial Arts.

Todman, Tonia. *Tonia Todman's Paper-Making Book*. Rozelle, NSW, Australia G.A., 1992.

Watson, Donna. *101 Simple Ways to Be Good to Yourself*. Energy Press.

Available From SkillPath Publications

Self-Study Sourcebooks

Climbing the Corporate Ladder: What You Need to Know and Do to Be a Promotable Person *by Barbara Pachter and Marjorie Brody*

Coping With Supervisory Nightmares: 12 Common Nightmares of Leadership and What You Can Do About Them *by Michael and Deborah Singer Dobson*

Discovering Your Purpose *by Ivy Haley*

Going for the Gold: Winning the Gold Medal for Financial Independence *by Lesley D. Bissett, CFP*

The Innovative Secretary *by Marlene Caroselli, Ed.D.*

Mastering the Art of Communication: Your Keys to Developing a More Effective Personal Style *by Michelle Fairfield Poley*

Organized for Success! 95 Tips for Taking Control of Your Time, Your Space, and Your Life *by Nanci McGraw*

P.E.R.S.U.A.D.E.: Communication Strategies That Move People to Action *by Marlene Caroselli, Ed.D.*

Productivity Power: 250 Great Ideas for Being More Productive *by Jim Temme*

Promoting Yourself: 50 Ways to Increase Your Prestige, Power, and Paycheck *by Marlene Caroselli, Ed.D.*

Proof Positive: How to Find Errors Before They Embarrass You *by Karen L. Anderson*

Risk-Taking: 50 Ways to Turn Risks Into Rewards *by Marlene Caroselli, Ed.D. and David Harris*

Stress Control: How You Can Find Relief From Life's Daily Stress *by Steve Bell*

The Technical Writer's Guide *by Robert McGraw*

Total Quality Customer Service: How to Make It Your Way of Life *by Jim Temme*

Write It Right! A Guide for Clear and Correct Writing *by Richard Andersen and Helene Hinis*

Handbooks

The ABC's of Empowered Teams: Building Blocks for Success *by Mark Towers*

Assert Yourself! Developing Power-Packed Communication Skills to Make Your Points Clearly, Confidently, and Persuasively *by Lisa Contini*

Breaking the Ice: How to Improve Your On-the-Spot Communication Skills *by Deborah Shouse*

The Care and Keeping of Customers: A Treasury of Facts, Tips, and Proven Techniques for Keeping Your Customers Coming BACK! *by Roy Lantz*

Challenging Change: Five Steps for Dealing With Change *by Holly DeForest and Mary Steinberg*

Dynamic Delegation: A Manager's Guide for Active Empowerment
by Mark Towers

Every Woman's Guide to Career Success *by Denise M. Dudley*

Great Openings and Closings: 28 Ways to Launch and Land Your Presentations With Punch, Power, and Pizazz *by Mari Pat Varga*

Hiring and Firing: What Every Manager Needs to Know
by Marlene Caroselli, Ed.D. with Laura Wyeth, Ms.Ed.

How to Be a More Effective Group Communicator: Finding Your Role and Boosting Your Confidence in Group Situations *by Deborah Shouse*

How to Deal With Difficult People *by Paul Friedman*

Learning to Laugh at Work: The Power of Humor in the Workplace
by Robert McGraw

Making Your Mark: How to Develop a Personal Marketing Plan for Becoming More Visible and More Appreciated at Work *by Deborah Shouse*

Meetings That Work *by Marlene Caroselli, Ed.D.*

The Mentoring Advantage: How to Help Your Career Soar to New Heights
by Pam Grout

Minding Your Business Manners: Etiquette Tips for Presenting Yourself Professionally in Every Business Situation *by Marjorie Brody and Barbara Pachter*

Misspeller's Guide *by Joel and Ruth Schroeder*

Motivation in the Workplace: How to Motivate Workers to Peak Performance and Productivity *by Barbara Fielder*

NameTags Plus: Games You Can Play When People Don't Know What to Say
by Deborah Shouse

Networking: How to Creatively Tap Your People Resources
by Colleen Clarke

New & Improved! 25 Ways to Be More Creative and More Effective
by Pam Grout

Power Write! A Practical Guide to Words That Work *by Helene Hinis*

Putting Anger to Work For You! *by Ruth and Joel Schroeder*

Reinventing Your Self: 28 Strategies for Coping With Change *by Mark Towers*

Saying "No" to Negativity: How to Manage Negativity in Yourself, Your Boss, and Your Co-Workers *by Zoie Kaye*

The Supervisor's Guide: The Everyday Guide to Coordinating People and Tasks
by Jerry Brown and Denise Dudley, Ph.D.

Taking Charge: A Personal Guide to Managing Projects and Priorities
by Michal E. Feder

Treasure Hunt: 10 Stepping Stones to a New and More Confident You!
by Pam Grout

A Winning Attitude: How to Develop Your Most Important Asset!
by Michelle Fairfield Poley

For more information, call 1-800-873-7545.